WHO MADE THESE TRACKS?

A Read & Learn Mystery

tangerine press
an imprint of
SCHOLASTIC
www.scholastic.com

Written by Tammi Salzano
Designed by Sandra Bruner

Copyright © 2009 Scholastic Inc.

an imprint of
SCHOLASTIC
www.scholastic.com

Scholastic and Tangerine Press and associated logos
are trademarks of Scholastic Inc.

Published by Tangerine Press, an imprint of Scholastic Inc.,
557 Broadway; New York, NY 10012

Scholastic Canada Ltd.
Markham, Ontario

Scholastic Australia Pty. Ltd
Gosford NSW

Scholastic New Zealand Ltd.
Greenmount, Auckland

10 9 8 7 6 5 4 3 2 1

ISBN-10: 0-545-17228-4
ISBN-13: 978-0-545-17228-8

Made in China

Words in **bold** can be found in the
Glossary on the inside back cover.

Animals make marks in the soft ground when they walk. These marks are called **tracks**.

You can find animal tracks in the sand, mud, dirt, and snow.

Do you know what different animal tracks look like?

Read the clues about the animals in this book.

Look at the picture of the tracks.

Then, see if you can guess the animal that made these tracks!

You can even make a rubbing of the tracks in this book. Put a piece of paper over the tracks. Rub them with a pencil. You just put animal tracks on your paper!

- I live in North America.

- I have dark fur around my eyes that looks like a mask.

- I can untie knots and open doorknobs!

- I dunk my food in water before I eat it.

- I like to eat small animals, fruit, insects, and even garbage.

Who made these tracks?

A raccoon

Mystery Animal 2

- I live in many places around the world. I am found in **deserts, tropical forests**, and even cold, snowy lands.

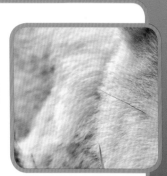

- I have long ears. They help me listen for animals that like to chase me.

- My fur is long and soft. It is brown, white, gray, black, or striped.

- I have strong back legs that help me jump.

- I eat grass and weeds.

Who made these tracks?

A rabbit

Mystery Animal

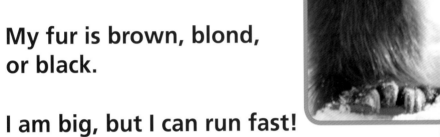

- I live in North America, Europe, and Asia.

- My fur is brown, blond, or black.

- I am big, but I can run fast!

- I like to come out of my home at night.

- I eat fish, berries, and small animals.

Who made these tracks?

A brown bear

Mystery Animal

- I live in many places around the world.

- My fur is brown. I have a white tail, too.

- I can hear and smell very well.

- I have horns on top of my head called **antlers**.

- I eat grass, leaves, and berries.

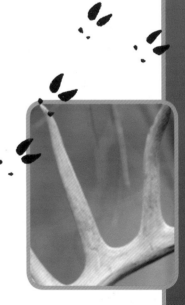

Who made these tracks?

A deer

Mystery Animal

- I live in warm waters around the world.

- I have a hard shell around me that keeps my soft body safe.

- Animals like me can weigh up to 700 pounds (317.5 kilograms).

- I can sleep underwater!

- When I was young I ate small animals, like shrimp and crabs. Now, I eat sea grass.

Who made these tracks?

A sea turtle

Mystery Animal 6

- I live in many places around the world. You can find me in the **desert**, the **grasslands**, and even where it snows.

- My fur is thick and warm. I have a long, bushy tail, too.

- I can hear and smell very well.

- I sleep curled up. I wrap my tail around my nose and feet to keep warm.

- I eat small animals, fish, frogs, lizards, and insects.

Who made these tracks?

A fox

Mystery Animal 7

- I live near water, like swamps and canals.

- I have greenish-black, scaly skin.

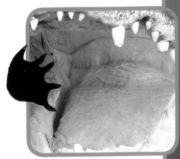

- My teeth grow back if I lose them.

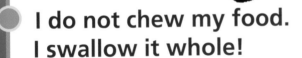

- I do not chew my food. I swallow it whole!

- I eat large animals, birds, and fish.

Who made these tracks?

An alligator

- I live in many places around the world.

- My skin is brown, black, white, pink, or patterned.

- I am smart. I can learn to do tricks!

- I like to roll in the mud to cool off.

- I eat plants and small animals, like worms and snakes.

Who made these tracks?

A pig

Mystery Animal

- I live in many places around the world.

- My fur can be different colors and patterns.

- Sometimes I sleep up to 20 hours a day!

- Many people keep animals like me as pets.

- I eat small animals, like mice and birds. I also eat store-bought food.

Who made these tracks?

A housecat

- I live in North America, Europe, and Russia.

- My fur is golden brown or black.

- I am the largest kind of deer.

- Even though I am big, I am a good swimmer.

- I eat grass, shrubs, plants, mosses, and pinecones.

Who made these tracks?

A moose

Mystery Animal

- I live in many places around the world.

- I have hair on my neck called a **mane**. I have a long tail, too.

- Some people keep animals like me as pets. I need a lot of room to run!

- I can sleep standing up.

- I eat plant leaves, stems, and hay.

Who made these tracks?

A horse

- I live in Africa and Asia.

- I have two large teeth called **tusks**. I use my tusks to dig and lift objects.

- My skin is thick, gray, and wrinkly.

- I flap my large ears to help me stay cool.

- I eat bark, fruit, grass and leaves.

Who made these tracks?

A sidewinder snake

Mystery Animal 14

- I live in many places around the world.

- My fur can be brown, black, white, or gray.

- I have long whiskers on my face. They help me to feel my way around objects.

- My teeth grow all the time! I have to chew on hard things to keep my teeth short.

- I eat all kinds of food, like insects, worms, fruit, and grass.

Who made these tracks?

A mouse